Out of the Darkness

My experience with depression

Virginia R. Conner

New Hope
Birmingham, Alabama

Scripture quotations indicated by TLB are taken from *The Living Bible*, copyright © 1971 by Tyndale House Publishers, Wheaton, IL. Used by permission.

Scripture quotations indicated by NKJV are taken from *The Holy Bible, New King James Version*, copyright © 1979, 1980, 1982 by Thomas Nelson, Inc., Nashville, TN. Used by permission.

New Hope
Birmingham, Alabama

© 1988 by New Hope
All rights reserved. Published 1988.
Printed in the United States of America.

N894102 • 5M • 0289

ISBN: 0-936625-62-7

Introduction

> Though I fall, I will rise again!
> When I sit in darkness,
> the Lord himself will be my Light. . . .
> God will bring me out of my darkness
> into the light,
> and I will see his goodness.
> Micah 7:8, 9 (TLB)

In Psalm 40 David reveals, "The Lord has brought me up out of a horrible pit." Today I can identify with David. Eight years ago I, too, was in a horrible pit. It was deep and dark and despairing and had the name *depression*.

For almost a year I wandered toward that pit. I didn't know where I was going or what was happening or why. When I finally stumbled into it, there was no way to change my course. The deeper I fell, the more I was blinded by the darkness. Finding my way alone was futile. I was so "deep-down" the only way out was with assistance.

While the depths of depression was like a pit, the journey into it was more like a tunnel. As I approached there were glimmers of light here and there, but they were followed by longer, lurking shadows. Warning signals flashed about me, but I did not see them. The tunnel of helplessness and hopelessness into which I traveled dimmed so slowly that I hardly noticed until the darkness overcame me.

Just as every tunnel has a core of darkness, so did my depression. Once I reached the depths that rendered me hopeless and helpless, I was forced to pause and examine my situation. Not until I admitted my need and called for help could I again move forward and my way begin to brighten. Only then could I begin to see the light at the end of the tunnel. The light was called *hope*.

For almost seven years I didn't admit my depression to others. I choose to write openly about it now in the hope of helping others who find themselves in the same darkness and despair. My most fervent prayer is that by sharing my experience, I will help others to cope by giving them some perspective on what is happening, some knowledge about the problem, and some course of action to take. Above all, I pray my experience will offer hope.

Into the darkness

More than the blues

Depression is no respecter of persons. It touches virtually everyone at some time. For some, it is a letdown feeling or a blue mood that may go with the weather or a minor disappointment. Sometimes depression doesn't seem to need a reason for being. It just is. It may last a few minutes, a few hours, a few days. Most importantly, depression doesn't last forever. You've experienced it before, and you will experience it again. It is temporary.

For thousands of others each year, there is another kind of depression. Its companions are an unexplained sadness, a lingering despair, a debilitating fear. You've never known such bewildering bondage. You wonder if the chains are permanent.

The blues, a dejected feeling, were nothing new to me. I think I had experienced them off and on most of my adult life. In particular, I could almost always count on postholiday blues. Like taxes, I dreaded them. I knew they were coming and thought the sooner I got them over with the better.

My husband dreaded them as much as I did because they were usually accompanied by crying spells. Too, I was never certain when they would come, how long they would last, or how they would take their toll.

One year the blues made their unwelcome appearance the day after Christmas in a foreboding cloud of gloom which hovered overhead, then dropped over me. Strangely, I don't remember tears, but rather a kind of paralyzing fear that pinned me down and held me on my bed. One thing was certain, this was more than a case of the blues. Even then I didn't recognize this feeling for what it was. Only through time and pain and experience did I recognize this as clinical depression.

Recognizing clinical depression

Clinical depression can reveal itself in a variety of forms. In me it found expression through severe anxiety.

While depression might be a sadness or worthless feelings about self and life in general, anxiety would be a constant state of worry and apprehension and feeling out of control of your life and the world about you. There is no doubt that in my experience anxiety and depression were incorporated. What happened to me the day after

Christmas was the culmination of a problem that had been building in me for at least a year and maybe longer.

Not until I entered therapy did I learn there exist three kinds of depression: physical, emotional, and spiritual. Several years before I had read the eight common symptoms of depression and had taken special note of them. Although they didn't all appear at once, for almost a year prior to my depression my journal records a progression from mild to severe sadness and apprehension in all three areas.

The down feelings I frequently recorded were followed by the same frequent resolves to overcome them. On one particular day my proposed solution was to "get really busy with housework." It didn't work.

Depressive symptoms should serve as a signal that something is wrong, but I didn't recognize the warning. They began early in the year and by the week after Christmas I'd had all eight symptoms. I first developed fatigue, then an inability to make decisions or concentrate, followed by low self-esteem (feeling worthless and guilty), inability to perform daily tasks, a severe weight loss, apathy toward my usual interests, a preoccupation with death, and sleeping too much. Some depressed people may eat too much or sleep too little.

The first warning signal came early the year of my depression and was physical in nature. On numerous occasions my husband admonished me, "Do you realize how often you complain of being tired?" I didn't. It was a subconscious response to a low energy level which gradually turned into fatigue and was probably my first cry for help.

My indecisiveness had always been a joke. "Don't give me two choices when one will do," I quipped. Yet I found myself wanting to make decisions less and less often.

Emotionally, many changes occurred during that same time period, changes over which I had no control. Some of them were minor and some quite serious. They all seemed to direct my thoughts backward to the past or inward to myself. I relived the past through regrets, lost opportunities, and feelings of failure. On my birthday I wrote a rhyme and put it in my journal beside a picture of myself at age 16:

> I think today of things that were and things that might have been, I think today of things that were and will never be again.

Pondering became a pastime that fed my anxiety.

Introspection produced low self-esteem, feelings of worthlessness, and an identity crisis. I constantly felt I did not do things well and, therefore, was a disappointment and bother to others as well as to myself.

In the proper course of time our sons had left home. The family had been the center of my adult life. The time to let go came sooner than I expected and was harder than I imagined. I wondered what kind of mother I had been to my sons. In particular, I wondered what kind of Christian mother I was to them. "Train up a child in the way he should go" especially pricked my conscience. I had taught them to be good. Had I taught them to be godly?

And what of myself now? Who was I? What was I supposed to be doing? Going back to school or finding a job seemed options, but not solutions. Not then.

The changes that dealt the hardest blow were the permanent ones. Early that same year, before my depression, an aunt died. My thoughts turned to my mother and my childhood home. They were gone. I wanted to relive some of the early pleasant childhood memories. I accepted an invitation to visit another aunt and in one afternoon attempted an impossible journey into the past.

I enjoyed the visit and being able to walk again through the large rooms of my father's family home. I enjoyed being with my cousins and aunt again and seeing the old barn, the walnut and mimosa trees, the flower garden, and the wraparound porch. But when my aunt said she wanted to keep things the same for her daughter, my cousin quickly replied, "Well now, things aren't the same, are they?"

I knew what she meant because so many family members were gone. In my own spirit I once again felt the pull against the change I so dreaded.

As my depression continued, I questioned my relationship with God. Did He love me? Why didn't He chasten me? Did I love Him? Was I obedient enough? I bought a new Bible and began to mark in red every reference to obedience I could find.

I doubted my salvation and assumed a burden of guilt and concern for others that went beyond family and friends to people I didn't know and would never see. It was a burden that was never intended for me, but one that had already been borne by God's Son on a cross 2,000 years ago.

Near the end of summer, preparation for our 25th wedding anniversary gave me a new interest and renewed energy. I decided to see a doctor anyway. He treated me for hypoglycemia, also called low blood sugar. It is best described as the opposite of diabetes. A diabetic burns blood sugar too slowly. The hypoglycemic burns it too quickly and becomes tired and nervous, weak or faint. The condition is aggravated by consuming high carbohydrates, usually in the form of sugar.

My doctor improved my diet and recommended a regular walking program. I started to feel even better, as if I had been given a fresh start, a new lease on life.

Then, like bookends around our anniversary, sadness struck. Two weeks before our celebration another aunt died suddenly. Two weeks following our anniversary, my doctor, his wife, and young son were killed in an accident. She had served at our anniversary reception.

The sudden losses were not the source of my depression, but they did act as a triggering device.

As time passed, I didn't grieve. Instead, I became morbid and preoccupied with death. Going to a hospital or funeral home was unbearable. If I went out of necessity, I felt death surrounded me. I became withdrawn, clinging to my husband.

There was no joy that Christmas. The beginning of the season produced its own brand of anxiety. The parties I usually enjoyed instead depressed me. I found them to be a frivolous waste of time. I was angry at those who in their merrymaking seemed to selfishly neglect the One Who was the purpose for the season.

The worst time came when my husband and I made our traditional one-day shopping trip. Each year I would complete as much Christmas shopping as I could alone. Then we would set aside a day to finish the shopping the two of us needed to do together. I always looked forward to that day because it was more than just another shopping trip. It was a special time of being together and usually ended with dinner and sometimes a show.

During the course of the day we had separated for individual shopping with a prearranged time and place to meet later. We are both unusually punctual people. As the meeting time came, 5 minutes went by, then 10 minutes, and 20. No husband. My imagination got out of control. Where was he? Had something happened? What was I to do?

I sat panic-stricken, huddled alone on a bench in the middle of a busy mall, clutching a scrap of paper in my pocket. As I looked up I saw my husband walking toward me. With him was a good friend and former church staff member we hadn't seen in a long time.

The paper in my pocket contained words I had copied that same morning from Psalm 73:26

(NKJV): "My flesh and my heart fail; but God is the strength of my heart and my portion forever."

Though suppressed, my hope in God struggled for expression.

The darkness

Some people say the emotional pain of clinical depression is more severe than physical pain. It can also be as crippling. My personal pain worsened the day after Christmas. A good friend reminded me, "Christmas has always been hard on you." The year of my depression I felt everyone else's happiness depended on me and what gifts I gave and the kind and quantity of food I put on the table. The expectancy of it all built to such a pitch and ended so abruptly that afterward there was no way to go but down.

By Christmas I'd had four symptoms of depression. The other four came in rapid succession in a matter of days.

I wrote in my journal that it was the worst Christmas ever. Now I don't believe it was. I do believe that was how I perceived it. The holiday season had the misfortune to be tacked on to a year full of painful events.

The pain that intensified the day after Christmas extended into the following week. I rarely got off my bed. I barely functioned.

Somehow I managed to keep my husband's clothes clean and put food on the table for him at night. I hardly remember doing either.

Weight gain was usually a holiday problem. That year, even though I was virtually inactive, weight seemed to pour off me.

Always an avid reader, with a sizable library of my own, I could no longer read—not even the Bible. And I could not watch television. All these things heightened my emotional pain and brought the hopelessness of the world into my home. Everything I saw or heard seemed to pass some kind of judgment on me and the world about me.

Besides no books, no newspapers, no television, and no radio, there was no conversation. Words stuck in my throat. Thankfully the phone didn't ring. Since I couldn't talk, and he wanted to keep me from my morbid thoughts, my husband played cards with me at night. Humor, if there was any, came in the number of times I won at rummy.

The climax and depth of my depression came cloaked in morbid gloom. On those cold winter evenings I looked into the coals in the fireplace and all I could see with my mind's eye was hell's lake of fire. I became consumed with the hopelessness of man without the Saviour God provided in His Son Jesus. I thought of the finality of death and the irreversible choices man makes for himself. Thoughts of death or dying occupied every waking moment.

Day and night, relief came only in merciful snatches of sleep. I could not get enough sleep, but I could not stay asleep. Sleeping was the only time I wasn't thinking, the only time I wasn't in pain. I had to stop thinking. Perhaps that is why some people begin to entertain thoughts of suicide. If momentary sleep relieves pain, perhaps eternal sleep would cure it.

We must understand that most people who commit suicide are in a deeply troubled state of mind and would not consider such a thing if their thinking were clear and time could pass.

If suicide crossed my mind, it kept going. I won't speculate on what might have happened under different circumstances or if I had rejected treatment. I didn't know how long I could tolerate the pain, but I was concerned about meeting God in that state of mind.

I once heard someone say, "We don't take our lives. We commit them to God." That was what I wanted—a deeper commitment to God.

Out of the darkness

Getting help

My depression persisted as the holidays passed. I waited too long before getting help. I had too many symptoms over a prolonged period of time that lapsed into months. Each new symptom was a signal I ignored. Early attention probably would have prevented the debilitation that resulted after Christmas. Any depression lasting more than a few days to two weeks demands attention. For some reason, with each new day I thought the symptoms would subside. They didn't. Delay was foolish and dangerous.

I should have known better. My husband is a pharmacist who deals medically and psychologically with people on a daily basis. Together we should have recognized the severity of my problem. Perhaps we were too close to it.

Interestingly, this wasn't my first experience with clinical depression. Twenty years before I had suffered from what was diagnosed as reactive depression—grief resulting from a loss. The circumstances, symptoms, and causes were different; and while I was melancholy, I was not disabled.

The reactive depression resulted from years of bottled up and denied grief. The loss of my father when I was 11 left a void in my life at a time when I really needed him. I thought I understood and accepted what happened; but in my teens I blamed every insecurity, every disappointment, every lost dream on his untimely death.

In the second and third years of my marriage, I lost two unborn babies. One was especially traumatic because I was four months pregnant. I didn't allow myself to grieve properly. Several years after the miscarriages, I still looked to people I admired and considered strong, like Jackie Kennedy, and thought I was in good company and that I too was strong. In reality, it was the worst thing I could have done. I had to learn that God gave us the healthy ability to grieve as an escape mechanism. One purpose of grief is to heal, cleanse, and release.

My second depression proved unique in that my therapist said he thought I did indeed grieve and that I did it all the time. He said if I had to do it all at once, I would not be able to bear it.

The reactive depression of suppressed grief 20 years ago took the form of frustration and guilt. My psychiatrist at that time called it anger—an anger turned inward. The second depression, the anxiety depression, was different. With it I felt submissive—humble and meek—like a lamb.

On a radio program, a Christian author remarked, "Depression is likened to a sheep 'cast down,' who cannot get up until he is helped by another." The first step I took in getting help was picking up the phone.

On a television program about depression I heard a woman say the hardest thing she ever did was to make the initial call for professional help. For me it was just the opposite. I had stopped functioning. I felt paralyzed. I had to have help. When I recognized my problem and admitted my need, I welcomed the opportunity to make that call.

Ordinarily I might have called my husband, my doctor, or my pastor to decide where to go for professional help. I did call my husband for his approval and support. Until that point I had been indecisive. Then I knew not only what I wanted to do, but what I had to do.

Twenty years earlier I found I could not discuss spiritual matters with my psychiatrist. When I made feeble attempts to do so, he seemed to treat those concerns lightly or brush them aside. This time I knew my depression had many spiritual aspects. As a Christian I knew I needed and wanted a professional who was also a Christian. I knew a large church in a nearby city offered a trained counseling staff. That was the first call I made.

Even as I dialed the number, a wave of calm swept over me. Until then I hadn't realized that help was as close to me as my telephone.

I suppose it was my inability to concentrate, but I had a hard time recalling the details of our conversation. I do remember the tone of it was a comfort to me. I also remember the counselor as being kind and gracious and compassionate—just as I imagined Jesus would be.

For some reason I was surprised that he knew all the right questions to ask, questions like, Have you had recent weight loss when you weren't trying to lose weight? Such questions helped identify for him the symptoms of depression in me.

He wasn't in a hurry. He took his time. Our conversation lasted the better part of half an hour, as long as necessary to accomplish the purpose of help and reassurance. Before our call ended he prayed with me, asking that my healing begin even then. I felt an immediate release in my spirit. He had given me the ability to begin to cope.

He also gave me the names and numbers of three professionals. The first two were psychiatrists, a man and a woman. The third was a licensed counselor. All were Christians. I chose the third name and immediately called for an appointment.

Treatment

I cannot stress enough, however, the importance of seeing a medical doctor. In time, I had a physical and in addition to my therapist, saw one of the recommended psychiatrists for several short sessions.

My therapist informed me, "People have a built-in coping mechanism and when functioning properly, our lows are hardly noticed."

But apparently no one has been able to determine which comes first, the chemical imbalance or the depression. I believe a mild depression began in me first and then accelerated until there was a chemical imbalance I could not control. The psychiatrist diagnosed a chemical imbalance as part of my problem. Treatment meant combined talk therapy with an antidepressant medication.

I've never liked taking medicine. Sometimes my husband can't even persuade me to take an aspirin. But the chemical imbalance made medication a necessary part of my treatment.

With many prescription drugs there can be some side effects. Since the antidepressant made me prone to drowsiness, I was first given a low dosage which was gradually increased to give the desired results. After a couple of weeks the drowsiness disappeared.

At the beginning of my therapy, I took a psychological test.

"Your anxieties came through in your tests, but you are healthy," my therapist assured me. I learned that with extreme depression a person could be emotionally disabled for a time and still be competent, but that if neglected indefinitely, one could eventually lose touch with reality. And, of course, through neglect there is the grave danger of suicide.

My therapy sessions began three weeks after Christmas and one week following my call to the church counselor. My call to him, along with my appointment with the therapist, sustained me until the sessions started. They began with one session a week and were eventually reduced to one every two weeks and so on until they ended.

I remained on the medication for a longer period of time, but eventually it was also discontinued. Treatment should always be individually determined.

My actions were affirmed one month after I began therapy as I watched a family counselor on a television special. "All of us need to know that going for professional counseling is a sign of strength rather than weakness. We all hurt and need someone to talk to about it," he said.

The sessions

The initial visit is a time to determine several things. One of them is cost—therapy can be expensive. Usually there are several acceptable methods of payment. If a person does not have the means for payment, sometimes special arrangements can be made. In my case our medical insurance provided for a percentage of the cost after we paid the deductible.

Time is another thing we discussed. After the first visit, it should be possible to offer a probable time frame for treatment—weeks, months, or years. I don't remember the details of the time we discussed. It seems six months was mentioned. Those six months, however, stretched into two years and four months, a long time for which I accept partial responsibility.

Nearly every week when I went for my appointment, there was some difficulty, some crisis with which I had to deal. It might have been of a personal nature or something on the national or world scale. I took everything seriously and was filled with questions I needed answered.

My therapist and I were each reading Catherine Marshall's book *Meeting God at Every Turn*. Some of the chapters dealt with subjects like illness and grief. I learned it was all right to ask deep questions when my therapist likened mine to those Catherine Marshall asked not only throughout her book, but throughout her life. He also acknowledged that my deep thinking could become a strength and not a weakness. He realized I was still asking questions that went unanswered in therapy 20 years earlier.

> As I wander in my plight of life
> and find that all are filled with strife,
> I wonder who and why I am,
> Why some are saved,
> and some are damned?
> Why was man born?
> What is his creed?
> Why are lives filled with misery?
> Why do we search and hurt and mourn?
> Again, repeat, why were we born?
> Were we made to be just what we are,
> or should we seek the fartherest star,
> or be denied for dreaming dreams,
> Return to scheming crafty schemes?

The therapist

One of the most important people in the life of a depressed person is the professional helper. The first person you see may not be the right person for you at all. It could take several visits to determine whether this is a person you can relate to and who can relate to you with a minimum of discomfort and embarrassment. After all, physical, emotional, and spiritual health and well-being are at stake and some people give more thought to selecting a comfortable pair of shoes than they would to finding the right therapist.

As a word of caution, sometimes we read in the news about professional people who have misused and abused their position of trust. The result can be tragic for everyone involved. Choose someone you feel you can trust.

For me it was helpful to discuss portions of my sessions with my husband. In my opinion this should be voluntary and not put a strain on a relationship, thereby causing more problems.

For several weeks my husband drove me to my sessions. That was partly because I was too anxious to drive myself and partly because he wanted to do so.

We saw the therapist separately on the first visit. Later there were a few times we saw him together and additional times separately. Until I gained confidence in my new situation, knowing my husband was waiting outside the door for me was a positive factor.

For therapy to progress and have its desired results, several elements were needed—openness, honesty and trust. I needed someone I could trust with the most delicate issues of my life. As a Christian, my therapist showed the gifts of encouragement and counsel. He used these gifts from the first session.

That session was extremely painful for me as I walked verbally back through the weeks and months leading to my depression. I wanted to stay in control of my emotions, but I could not. In a combination of stress and relief, the dam of pent-up emotions burst. I wept openly.

In compassion, my therapist looked at me and said, "I don't usually give feedback on the first session, but you need it." Hearing my spiritual doubts and knowing I was a Christian, he added, "God is obligated to hold you." For the first time I felt undergirded by God's strength. Later I found numerous passages in the Bible of God holding one with His righteous right hand.

The most helpful aspect of counseling was the objectivity. Talk gave me insight and a point of view of my problem other than my own distorted one. It helped to put things into a realistic perspective, back into focus. It also helped me regain my self-worth and self-confidence.

Talk and tears provided a release from my emotions and immediately began a cleansing and healing process in me. The ability to cope was joined by the promise of hope.

Support group

The chosen professional is one of several people in a needed support group. The understanding and help of some family members and friends is essential.

My husband was my mainstay from beginning to end. We married young. He had seen me through many struggles. He knew me better than anyone else.

In my depression, he was patient with my limitations and kind in my need. He never complained. Before therapy ended, I did see him grow weary to the point of impatience, but so did I. Most importantly, he never gave up on me or condemned me. The morning we left for my first session, he prayed that this would be the time, place, and person to help me. He also prayed for my healing to begin.

His presence and endurance were a comfort. One day he brought me a card. On the front was a picture of a cowboy and his horse hanging by a rope off the side of a cliff. Inside the card were the words, "Hang on, 'ol Buddy." These kinds of gestures by him helped to bring back a sense of humor and indeed kept me hanging on.

Before all this happened, our older son had married and was in his own home in a nearby town. Our younger son was living out of the state. We couldn't see that it would accomplish any purpose to tell them.

Although it has begun to change, for some reason in some circles there has been a stigma attached to psychotherapy. Depression, referred to by some as the common cold of mental health, may not be as readily identified as a broken bone. However, it should no more be neglected than a broken arm or leg.

Perhaps it was the prospect of the dreaded stigma, or perhaps it was simple embarrassment, but I didn't want anyone to know. Now I realize I probably could not have coped having people look and wonder, or worse yet ask. I realize too that in writing about it I make myself vulnerable and may not be able to answer some questions for some people.

There were two special friends who did know eventually. One was a lifelong friend who knew me better than anyone other than my husband. As soon as she learned what had happened, she sent a note of encouragement to me with the paraphrase of John 1:5, "God is light and in Him is no darkness at all." The passage was not a coincidence.

June lived near my therapist's office and we met often for lunch. If sessions were scheduled late in the day, and I dreaded the traffic, she would meet me and we would visit over coffee until the rush hour ended. She listened to the account of my sessions, as much as I wanted to tell. Even though she knew me well, she loved me anyway.

Mrs. Johnson was an older friend whose relationship with the Lord had grown rich with the years. She had an open prayer line and used it. I was humbled when she said she had wondered why she was in that place at that time and maybe it was for me.

This woman was like a spiritual mother to me, not that she led me to the Lord, but that she nurtured me in Him by her experience and example. I wanted to be like her as I grew in the Lord and in my service to Him.

These two friends offered the support of listening when needed or silence when necessary. They never judged me. They never gave unasked for advice. They did offer prayer, availability and, again, hope.

A third friend was a unique kind. She could sense a need and respond without having to know the problem. At the onset of my depression I was teaching a Sunday Bible class. The first Sunday I stood to face my class I was pale, gaunt, and strained. The following week my friend, who was also my class president, sent me a card with the phrase, "God is always there to lighten your way and lead you through 'darkness.'" An added note read, "From someone who cares for you." It was signed, "Wanda."

I was fortunate to have such caring and loving friends. I also had a great and loving God. In the midst of my depression I felt lost to Him. I couldn't find Him as I stumbled in the darkness. I was sure He had abandoned me.

When my therapist mentioned Him "holding me," it was as if the first small candle had been lighted. I can look back now and see with the anonymous writer of "Footprints," that when I thought I walked the darkness alone, it was God Himself who carried me in His arms.

Although the Lord's Word became an added support to me, my return to it was slow and in brief passages. His first word to me was from Micah 7:8 from a box of Scripture cards in my kitchen windowsill. His word was direct and specific: "When I fall, I shall arise; when I sit in darkness, the Lord shall be a light to me."

I had never been in such darkness, yet from every possible verse in the Bible, God had chosen this one and told me that even while I was still in the darkness, He would be my light.

When I went to my Bible for further reading, I found the added promise, "He would bring me out of my darkness and I would see His goodness" (Mic. 7:9, my paraphrase). I couldn't know then that God was preparing that verse for the theme of a book. It became my theme of hope.

Causes

I don't know when the root of depression was first planted in me. Early childhood can be a factor. In research I learned that loss of a mother can cause depression in an infant. My natural mother died the day after I was born. I don't know what kind of nurturing I received in the interceding days until I was placed with my adoptive parents.

My husband observed, "Several children may grow up in the same environment, and years later there will be as many views and responses to that environment as there were children involved."

In every home and with every child there are positives and negatives. I think I responded to the negatives—the don'ts, the shouldn'ts, the can'ts. Even in adulthood I have a need to please and be accepted. My therapist noticed a special need in me to be a help and to be affirmed.

While experts tell us anyone can become depressed, not everyone is prone to it. Women, however, may be more prone because of their unique caring nature.

It has long been thought that menopause and depression were related. Recent studies disprove that theory. In fact, the common age for depression today is in the 30s. That may be because of modern-day pressures on that age group.

My two depressions came in my early 20s and early 40s. My husband teased me, "You have never done things like other people. There is no reason you should begin now."

As a woman I believe I had a midlife crisis. The Bible mentions a normal life span as being 70 years. Using that as a basis, 35 would be the beginning of middle age. In my early 40s I questioned, Was my life half over? I began to mourn some of the things I had done and some of the things I had not done. I knew what counted in life was not possessions or money, but the eternal. Could I leave my children a spiritual legacy? What did my life count for up to now?

I read in the Bible from the book of James about life being a mist and vapor. I penned in the margin of my Bible the desire of my heart.

> Lord, I want my life
>   to count for You
> Not just some mist or vapor
>   quickly gone
> But one in service, praise and prayer
>   made strong
> And not for time alone
>   But for eternity.

In another way my crisis had nothing to do with age but with circumstance. I married the summer I graduated from high school. A year and a half later, one week after my 19th birthday, our first son was born. Two years later our second son was born. By the time they graduated from high school and entered college, I was still in my 30s. Once they left, they never seemed to come completely home again. I wasn't prepared for an empty nest just as motherhood fit so comfortably and motherly wisdom came more readily.

I believe temperament also helped set the stage for my depression. I had read Tim LaHaye's *Spirit-Controlled Temperament* before my depression and again afterward. The book brought great insight into myself and how I respond to life's issues. Immediately I recognized myself in his description of the melancholy temperament. The melancholic, according to LaHaye, has a rich temperament. She is analytical, self-sacrificing, gifted, and sensitive to emotions. Indeed, the emotions predominate and she can be ecstatic or gloomy and withdrawn.[1]

Though the melancholic can be moody, pessimistic, and vengeful, she is in good company with creative people such as artists, philosophers, and musicians; and biblical people such as Moses, Elijah, and the Apostle John.[2]

I also learned I had much natural potential when energized by the Holy Spirit. My greatest needs were the love, joy, goodness, peace, faith, and self-control which are the fruits of the Holy Spirit.[3]

As I understood my temperament and learned it was from God, and what He could do with it, I became more comfortable with it and with myself. I concluded that even with the pain derived from the sensitive nature of the melancholic, I would not change it. I would rather have the pain than to have a hard heart or less compassion.

Twenty years before with my first depression I described it differently.

> Afraid of life?
> Sometimes I am.
> Afraid of pain and want and death,
> But these are part of life itself.
> How much better I would know all three
> Than miss the blessing of the one.

---

[1]Tim LaHaye, *Spirit-Controlled Temperament* (Wheaton, IL: Tyndale House Publishers, Inc., 1981), 18.
[2]Ibid., 19.
[3]Ibid., 40.

Into the light

Not alone

As people have gradually learned of my depression their response has been amazing. "I can't imagine you being depressed. You're always so happy."

I was good at masking my feelings in public. Since I am rather quiet by nature, people didn't notice when I became even quieter. Some people thought my life had always been perfect. Others thought my faith could have been a shield against depression.

Being a Christian didn't exempt me from depression. It was a comfort to know I was not alone. Many godly men and women have suffered from its malaise. In the Old Testament, people who loved and served God became so depressed that in the midst of their ministry they cried aloud wishing to die.

The year after therapy ended, I stood in Israel on Mount Carmel remembering the prophet Elijah and his mountaintop victory followed immediately by his valley of despair. He had witnessed supernatural feats as God confounded and destroyed the prophets of the pagan god

Baal. But the victory was short-lived for Elijah when he was threatened by Queen Jezebel and literally had to run for his life. The stress of fear coupled with exhaustion, hunger, and doubt quickly produced depression in him. Enveloped in self-pity, Elijah begged to die until God provided rest, nourishment, and restoration of his sound mind.

James 5:17 (my paraphrase) calls Elijah "a man with a nature like our own." Our victories or defeats may not be as dramatic as Elijah's, but it is a source of help to identify with his humanness in them.

Some of the contemporary Christian writers who have meant something to me—Jamie Buckingham, Karen Burton Mains, Bill Kinnaird, and Sherwood Wirt—have mentioned in their writing their own "dark night of the soul."

God doesn't disown us because of our depression. In fact, when it is over, we find that He was with us in it, saw us through it, and brought us out of it stronger and victorious and ready to move on for Him.

To move on I had to recall the basis of my faith as I expressed it in a brief testimony years before.

> The despair of the cross
>   became the victory
> The darkness of the hour

    turned to light.
The tomb that smelled of death
    took on the fragrance of new life
As Jesus overcame
    everything I ever feared
He bought my soul
    and cleansed my heart
    and changed my life.

Many times I've heard people say, "I don't know how anyone makes it without the Lord." I doubt I could have.

I always wanted to do things the right way. When I made my profession of faith as a child I wanted to have a clear understanding of what it really meant to "believe on the Lord Jesus Christ." One definition I found for the word *believe* was to "lean heavily on."

A number of times I've mentioned the word *hopeless*. I can't imagine a worse feeling in the world than that of hopelessness—the despairing knowledge that nothing can be done. But nothing can revive a person's drooping spirit quicker than the words, "Yes, there is hope."

Jesus is the Risen Hope for hopeless man. Everything I base my life upon is tied up in the hope I have in my Risen, Living Lord as He is revealed to me in the Scriptures and by the Holy Spirit.

My therapist pointed out to me that all the time I thought I was sinking in despair, I never let go of Jesus. Even when I didn't realize it, I was clinging to Him.

When my faint cry was a mere "Help me, Lord," He was my life raft. The longer I held on, the brighter the light of hope on the rim of the horizon became.

By the time therapy ended I was ready to get on with my life. I was grateful for the help that was available when I needed it. It had occurred to me that I might make a once-a-year appointment to touch base, just as someone would make an appointment with their medical doctor for an annual check-up. I never did. The Lord had been with me in my crisis. I felt He now became my counselor. He began His ongoing therapy in me as He brought changes into my life and taught me about Himself and how to depend on Him through those changes. In fact, it was in those changes I discovered God's antidote for depression—looking to Him, not myself.

Changes

For changes to work there must be a yielding of one's life to Him. In a prayer poem I petitioned:

Change me, Lord.
Begin in the corners of my pride

for out of pride
the worst sins grow.
Work, too, on my obedience
for I want Thy will
but done my way.

I wanted to be a vessel for God, fashioned from a plain piece of clay into useful service and perfected into the likeness of His Son Jesus. The clay on the potter's wheel must be kept moist with water. I was thirsty for more of the Lord. I gave Him permission to use any means necessary to accomplish His purpose in the shaping of my life.

I believe depression worked as a potter's tool for change in me because I let it. I see myself and who I am in Christ in a different way. The doubts of salvation forced me to examine my faith. I am His workmanship, and just as a potter works on a piece of clay perfecting it, I know He is still working on me to perfect what concerns me. And He will never forsake me or give up on me. I am the work of His hand—His work of art, His masterpiece.

He has changed the way I see others by letting me see how much He loved me by the sacrifice of His Son. If He loves me, then He loves others just as much. If He worked in my life, He will work in other lives also.

Henri Nouwen coined a phrase and meaning

with his book title *The Wounded Healer*. The suffering and difficulties of our lives enable us to be wounded healers, helping others because we know and understand their suffering firsthand.

As a Christian I don't believe anything can come into my life without God's permission. Not everything that touches my life is good, but I believe everything can work for good because I love Him and He has a purpose for my life.

Sometimes I have to struggle against the struggles. I've learned it only intensifies the pain and the circumstance to pull against what God allows in my life. My circumstances can be a gardening tool in my Christian growth, in His perfecting of me. A vine cannot be fruitful without severe pruning at certain times. When I hear someone use the word *but* I know they are about to pull against their circumstances and against God's using their circumstances for good for them. The process is growth.

To relinquish my circumstances to God and to grow in Him is to realize that God alone is my Source. As someone said, "He makes the changes and they aren't always easy. They are always perfect." I can trust Him. He sees my life from the vantage point of eternity. He knows what is best. He is always right.

Listening and waiting

God changed the way I listen to Him. Usually it is through the Scriptures. He got my attention with Micah 7:8. He tuned my ear to hear His voice. Nothing calms a distressed sheep like the voice of the shepherd.

In therapy God knew I needed the joy of my salvation restored. One day as I turned through the Psalms, the only verses I saw were the joy verses. I took a pen and paper and wrote them down as fast as they came. They were a balm to my wounded spirit.

The year before therapy ended, I was admonished by Mark 6:31 (NKJV) to "come aside . . . and rest a while." I resigned my Bible class with the intention of returning after a year. I still have not returned to teaching. God changed my circumstances and removed me from my home church to a little mountain chapel we attend on weekends.

When I began teaching an adult Bible class I answered the call, "Feed My sheep." The call was changed to "Feed the sheep of your own household." By the time therapy ended our younger son had moved back home. I felt I was to make myself available to my family's needs and to my husband's schedule and to be flexible in my daily routine for Bible study, prayer, and praise (fellowship) with the Lord. I was not to take on projects that would confine me by making demands on me or taking great blocks of my time. By His Word, He continually impressed on me that I was to "rest in Him, be still before Him, wait on Him."

After therapy the hardest part was the waiting. But almost always waiting time is learning time, a time of preparation. I stopped being a distressed sheep and became a restless one. "Lord, when will You restore my ministry? What do You want me to do now? Are You there, Lord?"

Two years later, sitting in the quietness of the mountain chapel, His Spirit spoke to me: "Virginia, whether you know it or not, I am working in your life. I've called you for a time to be still before Me. For the time you cannot see, you must wait in faith. When you think negative thoughts, you must remember they are not of Me. When you are afraid you must remember that I've said unto you 'fear not.' Fear is not of Me.

"I am going to pour you out a blessing, but it is not my desire and not in My purpose to tell you when. You are to trust Me.

"Keep your eyes on Me. You tend to look off. You are going to have to learn to seek My face in all things—especially in the things that cause you worry and fear. Remember, I am the Author and Finisher of your faith, the Author of your salvation. Look to Me.

"You are going in the right direction even though to you it doesn't seem so and though it seems slow. Remember, time is not to you what it is to Me. Your time is not running out. I've seen your life from before its beginning. I knew what you would go through. I knew your searching heart.

"You're not perfect. You have a way to go, but, remember, you are Mine. I will never let you go. Trust Me."

Praising and praying

Charles Stanley's sermon tape, *Waiting on the Lord*, instructed me, as a restless sheep, that waiting time meant not moving out into a ministry until God said move. But it didn't mean I had to sit and do nothing. Instead I was to do daily what the Lord put before me.

I claimed another promise from His Word (Isa. 61:3, my paraphrase), "I will give you the garment of praise for the spirit of heaviness." The spirit of heaviness was the encumbering spirit from the Christmas of my depression. God promised to remove that old rag from me and replace it with a beautiful new garment called praise.

Praise is worshiping God. To me true praise is

what I do because of God's attributes—Who and what He is and what He means to me. It is done out of love in an attitude of giving.

I looked for ways to praise Him. Singing is joyous praise. What I wouldn't dare do in the presence of others, I did at home alone and unrestrained, or alone in the car. In fact, the first therapy session I finally drove to alone, I softly sang hymns of assurance and praise all the way there. In praise, I've used familiar hymns and choruses and my own original songs.

The piano became an instrument of praise. Lessons I had taken 30 years before gave me enough background to begin again. Patty, my teacher, was a gifted young woman near the age of my own sons. I was blessed by her gift of music and with her gift of friendship.

The sacrifice of praise restored my joy. The joy of the Lord became my strength.

Prayer

One of the biggest changes was in my prayer life. I learned to talk to God as I would a trusted friend. I didn't have to use form, or "thees," or "thous." In fact, I was more comfortable in being myself. It didn't offend Him for me to say exactly how I felt about anything, good or bad. He already knew. The openness and honesty made me less reluctant to pray, and built the Father-child relationship I so wanted.

The posture of prayer also changed. That too became natural. Sometimes I would pace the floor, or sit normally, or kneel in humility, or lie prostrate on the floor in an act of contrition.

Sometimes I would pray with arms extended upward with open palms, a gesture of giving Him a sin or burden. Other times the same open-handedness represented receiving from Him, an answer, a gift or a blessing.

My reading habits changed as I let the Holy Spirit redirect my interests.

I kept a journal before, during, and after my depression. Journaling has long been an outlet for my moods and emotions while at the same time providing writing practice.

There are periods when I daily write lengthy prose. There are times when there are wide gaps, lapses of time. For me to have to keep a journal would be a chore and dispel the excitement of spontaneity. Writing for me is a pleasure often inspired. My own best thoughts would be lost without it.

Besides being an outlet of release, it is a record of places, people, and events I want to remember. Frequently I will include news clippings, letters, or other items of importance to me.

In my depression and afterward, my journal has allowed me to see progress in my life and God's plan unfolding in my life. It was a valuable source of reference in writing this book.

Seeing His goodness

Since my early teens a desire of my heart was to write. When therapy ended that desire was revived. I excelled in writing in high school, but more than 25 years later I didn't know if I could still write. To me, as a Christian, writing serves two purposes—to minister to others and to glorify God.

At the encouragement of my husband, my therapist, and my psychiatrist, I drove five hours alone into another state to attend my first Christian writers conference. I made the trip three consecutive years, a milestone for one who had such anxieties about driving.

After the conference several more years passed. The longer I tried to wait on God, the more I complained. "How long would You have me wait? What are You up to, Lord? Are You there?"

Finally in desperation I cried out, "Lord, I don't believe You want me anymore. My usefulness to You in a ministry is over." I felt somewhat resolved.

Several weeks later, almost without thinking, I prayed, "Lord, if You ever want me to write about my depression to help others, will You show me?" It was a specific sentence prayer which I immediately forgot.

A week later a call came from Birmingham. Would I consider writing a book about my experience with clinical depression? I was afraid of what people would think. I was afraid of my writing ability. But the Lord impressed on me that waiting time was over, moving time had come. "What I have told you in the dark, speak in the light" (Matt. 10:27, my paraphrase). I was to act in faith believing this was God's open door of opportunity to minister again. I was to trust and obey and leave the outcome to Him.

In retrospect

Writing this book has combined joy with strain. The joy was in the fulfillment of promised, poured-out blessing and the long awaited answer to prayer. The strain was accompanied by unexpected outside pressure and distractions. Then there was the greater strain of remembering old pain. I had to drag it out, linger in it, tread through it, and pray I would be better for having done so.

From the perspective of the distance of time,

it has been therapeutic and enlightening to review what the Lord had done and is doing from that day to this.

There are times He tells us to "forget the former things"—the past hurts, broken dreams, and lost opportunities—for "He will do, is doing a new thing" (Isa. 43:18, 19; my paraphrase) But, in Deuteronomy 32:7 (NKJV) He calls us to "remember the days of old"—what He has done.

Before I began this project God spoke to my heart through Isaiah 63:11-14 (NKJV):

> Then I remembered the days of old . . .
> Who brought [me] up out of the sea [of despair] . . .
> Who put His Holy Spirit within [me]
> . . .
> Who led [me] by the right hand . . .
> Dividing the water [of fear] before [me] . . .
> Who led me through the deep [tunnels]
> And the Spirit of the Lord causes [me] to rest.

Then I remembered from Isaiah 61:3 the purpose of giving the garment of praise for the spirit of heaviness was "that he might be glorified." The purpose and goal of writing for me was to glorify my Lord and my God by the testimony of what He had done in my life. What He had done for me, He could and would do for others.

Conclusion

On any given day any one of us may experience for a moment, a sadness, a moodiness, or a letdown feeling. I would be dishonest if I didn't admit that I've had many moments with the blues in the last eight years. Undoubtedly I will have many more. Fortunately they have been temporary and none of them have been serious. However, if they linger more than a day or two, it does occur to me, could my depression happen again?

No one experiences life exactly the same way as another. God deals with us individually through a variety of circumstances, personalities and stages of growth. He works in the midst of them all right to where we are this moment.

Jesus didn't say "I am *a* light." He said, "I am *the* light. . . . He who follows Me shall not walk in darkness, but have the light of life" (John 8:12 NKJV).

My sincere prayer is that He may bring many others out of their darkness to see His goodness and the light of His love.

Virginia R. Conner is a native of Villa Rica, Georgia. Married 33 years to a pharmacist, she is a homemaker. She and her husband have two sons, a daughter-in-law, and three grandsons. Besides family, she enjoys Bible study and teaching, reading, writing, music, travel, and needlepoint.

COPING WITH DEPRESSION

Walter C. Jackson III

Depression is a painful human process, and all of us encounter it in one of its many forms from time to time. From the most low-grade or blues-like depressions, to the medium depressions, and to the most intensive clinical depressions, almost every one of us can remember at one time or another being caught in its seemingly unshakable grip. However intense depression is when it comes to you, the pain will be more intense if you keep it to yourself. Its agony is more unbearable when we won't talk about it—not to ourselves, to God, or to anyone else at all.

In its worst forms depression is an intensely anxious, hopeless, helpless, powerless sensation of body, mind, and spirit. Those who experience it feel numb and lethargic. Some of us feel a deep sadness, are gripped by fear, and feel like hostages. We live in inner despair as if abandoned. We hate loneliness, yet behave in ways to create larger islands of loneliness in which we live daily.

Depression is a formidable antagonist when it strikes. Like a monsoon season of the spirit, depression comes often as a dismal drizzle, at other times like an endless downpour, but never without a longing for the sunshine of balanced emotional life to dry out the endless sequence of rain-filled days.

Depression is not always so easily identifiable. It sometimes presents itself in less painful forms. Mild depression may be experienced as a general anxiety, discouragement, apprehension, or simple fatigue. Most of us try to ignore signs of mild depression if we have any awareness of it at all. We have actually developed automatic responses to it. A little extra sleep, having a good cry, exercising vigorously, getting busy with housework, being good to ourselves by buying something we want, going to a movie, being with friends and just forgetting the unhappiness are some of the ways we successfully overcome mild depressions. These are, however, simply ways to postpone facing the effects of the depression—but usually only for a limited time.

A more direct approach to depression is to talk things out with a marriage partner, a trusted friend, or with a caring pastor. This is by far the best and most healing way to deal with mild depression. It is an excellent way to ward off a buildup of unresolved negative emotions. It is also the first step in dealing with deeper depressions.

Virginia Conner is an exemplary model for us.

Her story includes the courage to reach out, which may inspire those who read her story to "take heart," to speak out and ask for assistance. She honestly reports how long she put off reaching out for help. So many persons in the constant throes of low-grade or mild depression use a multitude of excuses to resist getting help.

The author's testimony is that putting it off only prolongs the pain and makes the grief of it all the more intense. We would do well to imitate her faith-inspiring, courageous, and spiritually healthful plan of seeking help through caring, knowledgeable Christians as soon as we suspect we are in depression's grip.

Virginia also remembers and recounts several events describing the medium stage of her depression. Her growing list of personal symptoms included a pervasive low self-esteem, growing inability to perform daily tasks, eating disorders, sleeping too little, being unable to concentrate, reduced ability to make everyday decisions, and growing apathy or loss of interest toward things that previously brought great joy to her.

Her story is important because it may help you to recognize the depressive spiral when it is happening to you. It also may help you to recognize the symptoms in your loved ones or friends.

There are at least three additional things of great value we may learn from her courageous story.

First, Virginia Conner was and is a committed Christian, a truth which did not give her special immunity from depression. Depression is one kind of rainfall that does descend upon both the just and the unjust. Christians would do well to make plans to care for themselves and for their loved ones who become depressed. Let no power on earth be able to hoodwink you into thinking that God will give us a special shield against depression just because of our faith.

Secondly, her depression became increasingly more complicated, and progressively worse as time wore on. Most depressions are like this. They have a history of growth that may be observed and identified. Depression does not just go away. Like other processes of falling ill, depressions present themselves early enough to be given early care. Getting help early may bring relief and cure more quickly. Early care may also lessen the extreme depth of the experience of the depression, and may even assist the person to develop and strengthen coping measures of great usefulness in the day-to-day battle with reoccurring episodes.

Early care also assists in the preparation of family and loved ones—both the human family and the family of faith—to be of maximum assistance when the full-phased depression strikes. Knowing how to respond helpfully in loving, Christian ways is important. So many would-be helpers make responses calculated to help themselves feel good and actually ignore the needs of the depressed person.

Finally, Virginia's testimony is vital because she chose to reach out to God, to her husband and family, to a pastoral counselor, and to the whole range of health-care professionals available to assist her with her depression. As a Christian, Virginia possessed the most useful source of help available—faith in Jesus Christ, Son of God, the Great Physician, Eternal Source of hope for all who believe in Him. She maintained that faith at every phase of her experience and treatment. However thin her own faith at any given moment, she found God to be trustworthy and faithful. And, she found her husband to be steadfast and loyal in her darkest hours—something she might have missed if she had withdrawn from him.

Virginia found a trusted counselor in a nearby church counseling service, and through that person a psychiatrist and other professionals of the healing community. And she had at least one friend who met with her often and to whom she could tell what was going on inside her heart and mind. Such a friend, if confidential and loving, is one of God's most valuable gifts.

Finding Help

What might you do if you experience the nagging symptoms of depression Virginia reports? How might you secure for yourself the kind of assistance Virginia received when she reached out for help? And, what if you are seeking help for a depressed friend? After all, Christian counselors are not to be found in every church; and all mental health workers do not work eagerly with ministers or respect a person's faith in God.

The best advice, whether you are seeking help for yourself or someone else, is to prepare in advance. Make a list of suitable caring helpers. Your pastor, Christian family doctors, or nearby pastoral counselors may help you make your list. Christian social workers or school counselors are also persons who are in touch with caring Christians possessing the appropriate training and skills. Some of these pastors, doctors, counselors, social workers, and school counselors may themselves be well equipped to deal skillfully with persons in low-grade and mild depressions.

After you complete your list, cultivate some of those persons to become helpers for depressed persons referred by your ministers and Christian physicians. If you find a suitable one or more, consider inviting them to be speakers or workshop leaders on such topics as stress, burnout, or depression and the Christian life for your church. They will have a chance to get to know you; and you will have the chance to know them and assess their suitability as referral persons for your friends who need such help.

If you have an emergency, use the pastors in your area with the best reputations as counselors or caring persons as referral sources. Let a pastor introduce you to the kind of health-care professional you may need. Call your Baptist hospital if there is one nearby and consult one of the chaplains, or call a pastoral counseling center in a nearby city. One of them will surely have an appropriate referral for you. You may also call the counseling services of your Baptist colleges or universities for referrals; call the counselors at the Sunday School Board;[1] call the Chaplains Commission of the Home Mission Board[1]—that commission endorses chaplains and pastoral counselors to using agencies and certifying bodies on behalf of Southern Baptists. They are able to list most if not all of the endorsed Southern Baptist counseling specialists in your area and will know them personally.

Do not neglect your personal physician, especially if you wish to enlist the aid of a psychiatrist. Your own personal physician is an excellent person to provide you with a suggestion. A practicing Christian psychiatrist would be your first resource; but a good second choice is a psychiatrist who, though not a Christian, respects a person's faith and encourages the use of that faith for healing and health.

Remember, depression has a way of amplifying our prejudices. The powers of evil work in and through depression to nudge you away from anyone who could help you. Society's healers who are Christians are to be cultivated as friends of the churches and their members; such persons who are not Christians are to be tenderly but steadfastly witnessed unto that they too may become full believers in Christ. Every pastor in every Southern Baptist church should know the whereabouts of such people in their communities, and be leading their people to pray for them and to witness to them regularly.

Being Aware of Reactionary Depression

Virginia's open testimony about her history is also very helpful. She lists some life events most likely to have contributed to her depression. Similar episodes in our own lives need early attention in an effort to prevent them from accumulating and prompting depressions in ourselves. First, Virginia's mother died a few days after her birth, and her father died in her 11th year. These early days of sadness left deep scars of bereavement. By themselves these events were grievous, but became potential depression contributors not only because they were part of her history but mostly because they were largely uncared for, as she testifies.

Virginia, though a Christian early in life, did not learn to grieve openly as the Scriptures teach. Her sadness became an increasing burden for her and not a process of life with which she had learned to cope successfully. This style of life is common among Southern Baptists and is probably the most frequent cause of depression among us.

And so, Virginia carried a large burden of unresolved grief from an early age. She increased that burden when her close friends died. Apparently, she still had not learned to deal with the stress of grief. Additional family members died, and then her personal grief grew more intense. Two of her own pregnancies miscarried; her children left home. By then the accumulation of unresolved grief must have been unbearable.

The remarkable part of this story is to be found

in the answer to the question, How was Virginia able to function at all with such a load of grief and unresolved sorrow? Her testimony is characteristically modest. She must be a person of steadfast faith in God to have been able to survive so long without debilitating depression. She must have been cared for and upheld by a faithful earthly family and by a steadfast family of faith to have been able to function in society with that much unresolved grief. Her stamina in the midst of these events—and massive symptoms—gives an outstanding testimony to the power of God through her faith in Jesus Christ for the sustaining grace enabling her to bear up under such emotional burdens. Could preventive measures and open, biblical based styles of grieving have assisted her in avoiding the reactive portions of her depression?

In all probability, Virginia was doomed to her reactive depression because of her inadequate methods of dealing with grief. By her own testimony she did not "allow herself to grieve properly." She later learned that just being strong is not enough. But she finally learned "that God gave us the healthy ability to grieve."

Like so many of us, she had been ashamed of her progressively ill sensations at the heart of her very being. She believed, falsely, that she, a

Christian, should have been able to carry any kind of burden and not become depressed. She believed with so many of our adult generation that emotional stress should be "handled." She was, unfortunately, committed to the unhealthy and thoroughly unchristian thought that believers in God are somehow protected from the rainfall of emotional illness, and that she should have been able to face her problems alone in prayer with victory.

Anyone in that frame of mind should consider the teachings of the Bible. There is a "time to weep, and a time to laugh; a time to mourn, and a time to dance" (Eccl. 3:4 KJV), and a time to be aware of the symptoms of pain and depression so eloquently described as having been experienced by the heroes in the Scriptures. "I am weary with my groaning; all the night make I my bed to swim; I water my couch with my tears" (Psalm 6:6 KJV). "Let the day perish wherein I was born. . . . My soul is weary of my life" (Job 3:3, 10:1 KJV). "My kinsfolk have failed, and my familiar friends have forgotten me. . . . My bone cleaveth to my skin and to my flesh, and I am escaped with the skin of my teeth" (Job 19:14, 20 KJV). Symptoms of depression are well known to the biblical writers. "Lover and friend hast thou put far from me, and mine acquaintance into darkness" (Psalm 88:18 KJV). "Reproach hath broken my heart; and I am full of heaviness: and I looked for some to take pity, but there was none; and for comforters, but found none" (Psalm 69:20 KJV).

The truth of the matter is that we probably do not have to endure the depth or the duration of reactive and clinical depressions that is frequently experienced. Early openness to family and Christian friends about matters that make us blue can lead us to discover the powerful spiritual truths about two or three gathered together in the Lord's name; and about the power of the prayers of a righteous believer making intercession for us. Developing adequate care for bereaved persons within the Christian family is a vital method of early care for depression in its formative stages.

And, when depression comes, it is not a stranger. It is only one brief episode of pain anticipated by our loved ones. They will be ready to help us. And the Lord is constantly ready—staying steadfastly by us until we learn in our own bodies, minds, and spirits the truth written by the psalmist who said, "For his anger endureth but a moment; in his favour is life: weeping may endure for a night, but joy cometh in the morning" (Psalm 30:5 KJV).

[1] Home Mission Board: (404) 898-7000; Sunday School Board: (615) 251-2000.

Walter C. Jackson III is Professor of Ministry, Southern Baptist Theological Seminary, Louisville; Kentucky.